People of the Passion
and
Mary M: A Visit With the Magdalene

Mary Betten

Sheed & Ward

Sheed & Ward™ is a service of National Catholic Reporter Publishing Company, Inc.

Library of Congress Catalog Card Number: 87-61922

ISBN: 1-55612-079-6

Published by: Sheed & Ward
115 E. Armour Blvd.
P.O. Box 414292
Kansas City, MO 64141-4292

To order, call: 1 (800) 333-7373

For
Muriel ~
With happy memories
of our visit and in
celebration of a new
of friendship
Nancy
Better

Contents

Mary M: A Visit With the Magdalene

For Patrick who is everything to me.

Acknowledgments:

For: Msgr. George Niederauer who helped me find my faith when I thought I'd lost it. Betsy Caprio who taught me to see stories in my shadow. Bob Lussier who found me the sweet support of Chant to fit beneath the words; and Rita K. Brown who challenged me to see comedy in scripture; and indefatigable Msgr. Richard Murray who commissioned me to write *People Of The Passion* for his parish and never stopped hounding me until I handed him the first character a year later; and for my Publisher, Bob Heyer who saw me perform *Mary Magdalene* at The Cathedral of St. John the Divine in New York in 1981 and called me in Thousand Oaks, California one Spring morning in 1987 to see how both of us were doing, and here we all are.

Foreword

Twice in the history of the West religious experience and ritual gave birth to the drama. Over 2500 years ago in Greece, pagan rites developed into the tragedy of Aeschylus, Sophocles, and Euripides, and the comedy of Aristophanes. This theatrical tradition died with the Roman empire, only to be reborn in the tenth century, when a few deacons, fully vested, processed into the sanctuary of a monastery chapel during Matins on Easter morning and imitated the women and the angels at the tomb of Jesus: "Whom do you seek?" "Jesus of Nazareth." "He is not here. He is risen." Once again, characters, dialogue, action, suspense and imitation of life—and in the sanctuary of a church!

Of course the sanctuary could not long contain this outburst. It moved into the body of the church, then into the churchyard, then to various locations throughout the towns. But always, for 600 years, it told the same story, the good news, from Creation to Last Judgment, along the way enlivening the stories with Mrs. Noah as a nagging wife, one of the Christmas shepherds tossed in a blanket, and an expense account for costumes, listing as one item, "God, all in white leather."

It was too good to last. Some humorless rulers suppressed religious drama, and the theater developed in other directions. They were magnificent directions, and they led to Shakespeare, Shaw, O'Neill and Eliot (himself no stranger to sanctuary, or chancel, drama). But still something was missing. Now it is returning to the drama and the Church, and Mary Betten is part of that tradition and that return. The dramatic monologues in this book call forth the same kinds of performances and discussions as those plays of long ago, springing from the good

news made accessible and interesting and entertaining to the human believers of the present
time.

But is the Church ready and willing for this
renewal of chancel drama? Just listen to the
fathers of the Second Vatican Council:

> Literature and the arts are also... of great
> importance to the life of the Church. For
> they strive to probe the unique nature of
> man, his problems, and his experiences
> as he struggles to perfect both himself
> and the world. They are preoccupied
> with revealing man's place in history and
> in the world, with illustrating his miser-
> ies and his joys, his needs and his
> strengths, and with foreshadowing a bet-
> ter life for him.
>
> Efforts must therefore be made so that
> those who practice these arts can feel
> that the Church gives recognition to

them in their activities, and so that, en-
joying an orderly freedom, they can es-
tablish smoother relations with the
Christian community. Let the Church al-
so acknowledge new forms of art which
are adapted to our age.... Adjusted in
their mode of expression and conformed
to liturgical requirements, they may be
introduced into the sanctuary when they
raise the mind to God. (*Pastoral Consti-
tution on the Church in the Modern
World,* #62)

That's it, exactly. These plays illustrate our
miseries and our joys, our needs and our
strengths, and foreshadow a better life for us,
and they do all this in a remarkable and valu-
able way. They connect our experiences and our
feelings with the people of the Gospel, the people who met Christ in the flesh, and who were
changed by that experience. Until now we have
seen and heard these people at a distance, in
stained glass, in a reading or a homily, and we

assumed we had nothing in common with them. They were a planet away from us in time, and maybe the Master they met seemed to be so, too.

Mary Betten tries to change all that. She takes us in for a close-up; she takes us inside Jairus's daughter, and we listen in on her feelings and her memories. The playwright puts flesh and blood on an ancient disciple, like the bride at Cana. She tells us stories, as Jesus did, but they are about the real people he touched and enthralled with those stories. In a way she helps us meditate in dramatic form, and as we interpret these dramatic moments, either aloud, in performace, or in silent reflection, the gospel narrative can come to life in a new way.

"Here is God's plenty" in his ways of dealing with his sons and daughters through his son, Jesus the Lord. We watch and listen as God surprises the well-ordered lives of people like the maiden and the mother, and we think of

God breaking into our carefully formed habits
and patterns and attitudes. Strong egos get challenged, and lives get changed around, whether
they want it or not; we listen to the silversmith
or the centurion, and we reflect on our own
need to control everyone and everything. In this
way, religious experience becomes faith experience when we recognize God's action and, after a struggle, finally respond with welcome, ac-
ceptance and change.

Do we secretly believe, though, that God
could never change us? We listen to Pilate's
wife and we meet a woman taking responsibility
for her own faith, and warning us that Jesus will
call us to do that, too. Is God's way always so
neat and sweet and orderly that he will just do it
all for us, making failure impossible? Listen to
the hell beginning in the woodcutter's rejection
of grace.

In all our Christian journeys, alone and
together, there are moments of breakthrough,

of recognition, and the more we listen to the Lord in prayer and reflect upon his presence and action in our lives, then the more ready we will be to perceive his action and presence, the difference he is making, and let go to it. Mary Betten makes these people human and approachable, these people whom Jesus approached, so that we become convinced it can happen to us, too. And it happens much more often than we are willing to admit. Just listen in while the shepherd's nephew does his double-take, and changes his whole understanding of life.

But the litmus personality in this collection is Mary Magdalene, "Mary M." She is a supreme example of someone falling in love with God, and she uses the language of passion, the only language familiar to her, to describe her chaste and total love for Jesus. Perhaps this language will bother us a bit, just as the tears and the hair and the ointment bothered Simon the Pharisee.

We hear what she did for love, and we reflect on what we have done, or would do.

Each of these people of Christ's passionate love has memories, fantasies, yearnings, thoughts, feelings, random images, and some very private sadness or joy and the grace of meeting Jesus Christ. So does each of us, and in these plays Mary Betten guides us in finding meaning and direction for ourselves in the experiences of our oldest brothers and sisters on the Christian journey. So enjoy the plays. But beware: as you look through the windows of these souls, you may spy a mirror or two.

—Most Reverend Roger M. Mahony
Archbishop of Los Angeles

People of the Passion

Introduction

These nine monologues can be performed by nine different people, or by one man and one woman or by one person as a dramatic reading.

The audience appreciates time for reflection after each monologue. This time can be filled with silence, the reflective movement of liturgical dance, or with music. Variations on the

1

melodies found in the Liber Usualis work well, played by a flute or similar wind instrument.

With a life-size crucifix as the focal point of the stage, a portable spot can be used to light both the performer and the crucifix, alternating from one to the other for the reflection time.

A contemporary black wardrobe is suggested for both performers and musician.

Two of the performers begin the play by coming center stage together near the crucifix.

Performer #1: speaks from Scripture:

"Jerusalem, Jerusalem, I would have gathered you as a Mother Hen gathers her chicks."

Performer #2:

"A story is told of a weathy mid-west farmer who raised beef cattle for market. One night a fire destroyed his entire farm, killing all the cattle and burning his home and barn to the ground. The next morning, as he walked about the devastation he spotted the burnt carcass of a mother hen. In depression and anger he kicked the charred carcass and from underneath came all her golden chicks running free into the world.

Performer #1:

"We dedicate this performance to Jesus, our Mother Hen, who died so that we might live."

The light goes off, music plays briefly and *People of the Passion* begins.

1.

The Servant Girl

I love the wheat fields. I could stand in them forever and feel the sun on my face. Sometimes when no one is looking I lie down in the warm wheat and watch it wave back and forth—tiny golden flags against the open sky. The countryside is my home. My Father sent me out for hire and my pay is sent back to him. I'm a servant here in the palace of Caiaphas in Jerusalem. It's been two years since I've seen

waving wheat or smelled the open air. I come
from Galilee. I miss the soft accents of my people there and their easy way of life. Our house
is near the sea of Galilee. The sea, like the
wheatfields, has a life and schedule all its own. I
think the sea even has its own people. I remember them from the mornings I'd rush to my
shutters and throw them open to the sounds of
Fishermen preparing their nets for the day.
Their work is a dance to the music of the sea.
Their talking and laughing is the song I miss.
Oh, and their jokes! Fishermen tell wonderful
jokes. They throw back their heads and laugh
into the wind. When I go to bed in my tiny, stuffy cubicle at the top of the palace I dream about
the sea. I see myself opening my shutters, I hear
the familiar voices and I feel safe. My Father
has promised I can come home at the end of
this year if I don't get in any trouble. It's hard to
stay indoors at night when my work is finished.
It's stuffy in my room, the air is so tight and
there is no one to talk to.

There was a wonderful man warming himself at the fire in the Courtyard last week. I knew two things about him when I heard his voice. He was a Fisherman and he was from Galilee. They were holding a Prisoner in the Palace who was arrested for what he preached and I had seen this man with him when he was preaching. I got so excited thinking I could identify someone by their accent; after all, it isn't very often anyone around here listens to me. It would be fun to feel important and most of all, the man might talk to me about home. So when I came out to the fire, to get his attention, I told everyone he was a friend of the Prisoner and he was from Galilee. He got angry so quickly and started shouting denials. There was a great disturbance. The other men around the fire yelled back and in the middle of the shouting and denying a cock even crowed in the courtyard. The man seemed to lose all sense of reason as though the Cock had called his name. Everything was bedlam. Word got back to my Father.

People Of The Passion

I won't be going home. And that man, that
gruff, wild, wonderful fisherman... my friend
from a distance... if only I could explain. I was
just acting on impulse, showing off... do you understand? I wish there was some way to let him
know I'm sorry.

The Servant Girl

2.

A Woodcutter

I work with trees. I go alone to cut them, always aware of how they breathe and drink the rain and catch loud sounds in their branches giving me back a sweet silence. When I chop I listen to the rhythm I make and think about my longings. The Romans pay me to bring down the Cypress tree in one piece, strip the branches and haul the bare posts into Jerusalem to be used for crucifixions. They pay me well. Once the Cypress is cut she never springs up again. But the Romans don't care.

The olive tree will grow again though, from the smallest graft or the oldest stump. She is a noble tree. But the waving Cypress is like a wanton woman, promising her beauty then leaving after one night. When I tear away her branches I think of the thieves and slaves who will feel her against their legs and die in shame. Sometimes I sing to the rhythm my chopping makes and my echo tells me: soon I'll be too old for my job, unable to lift the wood and stand straight. Yet the olive tree will rise again from the oldest stump while I will die. How proud I'd be to leave my mark on the tree of generations yet to come, but the law forbids cutting the olive tree. Like a valiant woman she toils, making light for the lamps, oil for anointing.

When I head back to Jerusalem the donkey pulls the poles slowly. Some are longer than others. I flex my hands and study the furrow the longest pole has made in the muddy road. I walk in the deep rut thinking of the sound the coins will make in my pouch when the gates of the city are behind me. It is April and the fruit trees' innocent blossoms peek from their buds reminding me it is Passover and the Pilgrims will be coming to the City. There is no time to spare. I must deliver the poles to the Romans and leave to avoid the crowds. There won't be time to drink my fill of wine and drown my longings.

With the coins safely in my pouch I make my way toward the gate knowing it will be difficult to get through. The crowd is surrounding three men on their way to be crucified. The Soldiers seem louder than usual and the crowd is an odd assortment. I see the first man stumble and fall and when I hear the soldiers' reaction, I fear what they might ask next, so I crouch down not to be noticed. They call louder for a strong man to come assist the condemned. I notice a tall, muscular man ahead of me. I push him forward, staying carefully hidden. They order the man I pushed to help carry the cross. I burrow my way through the people as they ask for his name. A deep voice booms, "Simon of Cyrene." "Help him" the soldiers yell, "he's the Messiah; it's an honor." The soldiers laugh, slapping each other on the back. I'm careful not to look at the face of the man who will eventually soil the Cypress. I'm almost free from this trap. Almost out the gate. An unknown force in my head begins chanting to the rhythm of my running; it is the same beat as my chopping sound. I feel the longing come over me: "Look back, look back, look at the man's face. Look at the man's face," but I run, ignoring the longing, pushing myself free. At last the gate is behind me. My own sense of order returns. Further down the road I see a new place has opened where I can drink my fill and forget. Tomorrow I'll head back to the forest, chop the same trees, get perhaps more money and sing my song of longing. I just do my job. But I wish there was more.

A Woodcutter

3.
Pilate's Wife

Probably I'm the only person you've ever met who can say, "all my dreams have come true." I've had three dreams in my life. The first started when I was 16 and kept reoccurring: I could fly! Did you ever dream you could fly? My diviner says flying dreams are normal in the teen years. Danger would get this close, and zoom, Away I'd fly. It was a secret gift.

The second dream came in my twenties. I rescued people form burning buildings. They would be completely engulfed in flames and somehow I'd save them. It was a feat beyond human strength and I loved the dream.

The third dream came after I was married. My husband, Pilate, the mighty Roman Procurator of Judea was judging a criminal from Nazareth who had claimed to be the King of the Jews. The man had been scourged and brought before him for his crime. I must assure you, my husband knows a great deal about crime. I have seen him disguise Roman soldiers as Jews, send them to mingle in the crowds, watch for a given signal, then turn and kill innocent Jews wantonly. I've watched him steal temple funds and spend sacred money on pet projects of his own, and once I even saw him order an attack on a religious procession of Jews. "They were dressed for dying," he said. He applauded how neatly they fell into the folds of their holy garments.

But this was all in his later years. When he had many chins, his brain gone, his heart turned to stone. When I married him he was lean and handsome, full of hope. I was the one who made it possible for him to be Procurator; as the grand-daughter of Caesar Augustus, I was even favored enough to follow him to his assignment. And so you see, in the beginning I watched all he did with a lively interest. When he judged the man from Nazareth, I sneaked down the back stairs from my chambers to have a look at the Criminal from between the curtains behind my husband's throne.

"Are you the King of the Jews?" my husband was yelling. No answer. "Are you the King of the Jews?" He became enraged with the silence, the back of his neck went red, his ears enflamed like tiny lanterns on either side of his head. The air was charged with challenge. The man's blood dripped on the flagstone. It was as though he were waiting for something. From the center of the curtains I stuck my head out further. The man from Nazareth slowly lifted his face till he met my eyes, raised his voice and said deliberately to me, "Thou has said it." I staggered backwards and dashed up the stairs and fell on my bed. How did he know I was there? Why was he talking to me? Voices reached me through my windows; they had taken him outside below my porch. Orders were given for a crown and a cloak for the King and then I think I fainted.

In my dream I looked down at him beneath the branches of a tree. The crown of thorns on his head were arms reaching up to me. The scarlet cloak on his torn shoulders set his body on fire and the peoples' arms reached higher and higher in the flames for me to save them. I knew he had the power to flee. "Fly away," I called to him. Yet he raised his head again to me, his eyes as soft and warm and full of promise as the April earth upon which he stood. It was my first experience of innocence. I had been born into power, manipulation, force, and yet I knew what he was telling me. This innocent, foolish man was going to die for me. Why? Why was he singling me out?

When I awoke I found my maid and said, "Go to my busband and repeat this message: 'I have had a dream, have nothing to do with this man, he is innocent.,'" It was too late. Pilate commanded that the man from Nazareth should die and from that day forward he had decreed his own death until finally he took his life by his own hand. I found my husband's body one dark night years later; he had slashed his wrists over a basin and washed his hands in his own blood. For countless nights, over and over again he had washed his hands, but this night was the last night. He lay beneath the basin slumped on the flagstone like an old army boot, ill-used, the laces missing, like his dreams vanished that April day so long ago. And since I've been introduced to the King of the Jews, and come to know the flight of innocence and the power to save, I have a message for you: Be careful what you dream. It may come true.

Pilate's Wife

4.

A Silversmith

I always thought I was a good husband and father until a desire for revenge came into my life and I set out to get even. Then I changed. I learned how to hate. I was a wealthy silversmith. I had my own business, built up with my own talents. I did intricate work in silver, I made idols and sold them mostly to tourists; they were expensive. My wife says people like my work because it shows the power of the gods. I keep the store well stocked. I work late every day. It's always dark when I close the door to go home to my wife. I guess you realize I haven't mentioned my child. My daughter...she is beautiful. And silent. She doesn't speak. She has never said a word in her life. I have often used her as a model for my idols but no one knows this. She is never near the shop. My wife keeps her, or I should say, my wife hides her, at home.

In all the years I've had my shop I've never missed one day of work. The doors are always open. One day my wife took me aside and said she had something very serious to discuss and begged me to understand. She began to explain. It became clear she thought our daughter had a chance to be cured. She had heard of a Nazarene who had cured a blind man who had been blind since birth. When she told me what she had heard him preach, I knew I could never believe it, but if my wife wanted me to go for our daughter, I knew I would do anything for her happiness. My work was with the idols and I could only believe in the strength of my own hands and the power of my own creations. That could never change. I mentioned none of this to my wife. I only told her I would go to hear the man. I looked at my daughter wrapped in her cloak of silence and I knew it was going to be difficult. One only gets what one works for.

The people gathered to hear the man on a steep hill. They seemed spellbound by the man's message. We had my daughter's face covered, as we seldom take her out in public. I feel confused but I remind myself my daughter is precious to me. I watch my wife listening and I know she believes; she hasn't told me but I can tell by the way she listens. I watch my daughter in her dumbness as the man speaks. She studies his lips. She seems to comprehend. The man is about 33, he is comforting to hear. I guard my thoughts and think of the money I am losing having my shop closed. The sun begins to grow faint. I know the crowd must be hungry yet no one moves on the hill. I don't even want to move. The words are powerful.

A young man about the age of my daughter approaches the speaker. He has a basket of fish and some loaves. The man continues speaking and begins to lift fish out of the basket. Fifty, 70, 100, 1,000 fishes and loaf upon loaf of bread come out of the basket as though there is no bottom. The boy's eyes grow wide, the people pass the loaves and fishes, there is laughter and singing. I am laughing and singing, my wife is singing, my daughter is singing. She hands me a fish. My daughter is singing!"You're speaking," I scream. "Drop the fish! You are singing." I toss her high into the sky. She is laughing, our laughter is music all over the hill. My wife cries softly with joy. We sit on the hill in the twilight surrounded by a sea of love. And the miracle of sound, and the miracle of the loaves, and the miracle of the fishes. And it is a day never to be equaled!

A Silversmith

When I approached the shop to open early the morning of my return, it was empty, completely empty. Everything I had ever made had been taken. I had been robbed while I sat on the hill. My life's work—not one piece left. My livelihood...gone. And so you see, revenge entered my heart driving out gratitude and joy and in its place a wild rage to find the thief. I wanted to kill him; I wanted him to die for making me a poor man, left with nothing.

The days passed and in time my wish came true. The day arrived for me to see the thief die. I was a poor man now but he would soon be a dead man. Crucified for his thieving deed, and I didn't have to touch him. The Romans found him and killed him for me and all I had to do was watch. The day of his execution arrived. Three men were to be crucified that day. I ran to his death, yelling, "Crucify him, let's see the dog die!" If the crowd yelled, I yelled louder and when they chanted death, I chanted it faster and faster. I waited to kick him and spit on him for what he had done and when I got up to the first man with the great beam on his back I opened my mouth and a wail came from my lips like a woman in labor. For there beneath my spit and screams was the Rabbi who had given my daughter a voice. A great hobnailed boot came down atop his grasping hand. On that kind hand that had reached out to the multitudes, touched a blind man's eyes and loosed my daughter's tongue into a song of praise one sunny afternoon.

I followed like a dog kicked out into the rain. My mind was numb. I stayed close. What was I to do but follow? I listened in case he would speak. There was little chance he would utter a word and yet, that afternoon on the hill everything had been so clear. Surely there would be a word from him to go on now.

They hung the Rabbi between two thieves. Toward the end I heard the Thief I had come to see ask the Rabbi to save him and I heard the answer, for I stood as close as I might stand.

The thief was told he would be with the Rabbi that day in Paradise. I stumbled home. I'm not sure to this day what happened to my revenge. I only know my daughter, my wife and I are disciples now. We travel with the Rabbi's followers and I preach. I tell about what I heard that day on the hill. But of what I heard that day on the cross, I'm unable to speak.

The Disciples call the Thief on the left the Good Thief. And when I think of him I smile. He was indeed a good thief to rid my shop of idols. We use the empty shop as a meeting place now—to break bread, to give thanks. And I am a rich man.

5.

The Bride of Cana

I have hair the color of new wine. My husband tells me that and then he kisses me; it's like a ritual with us. He is the most clever, most handsome man in the world. We've been married three years and I still tremble when I think of how much I love him. We grew up together in Cana and we'd still be there except my husband is so clever he got a wonderful job here in

Jerusalem and now he's a prosperous merchant and we have a two year old daughter. Our parents are proud of us. We go back to visit them once a month. My parents actually stop arguing when they see our daughter. I guess their arguing doesn't mean anything. They have always argued for as long as I can remember. On our wedding day they fought about how much wine to serve and it got so bad they wouldn't even speak to each other until finally it happened. We ran out of wine.

My mother ran behind the water jugs and wept, she was so embarrassed and ashamed of her temper. A friend of my Grandmother's came to comfort her. She said maybe her son could help. He was there with about a dozen of his friends from Nazareth. One of his friends was very loud and funny. I remember his name was Peter. We kept calling his name and clapping while he put a goblet of wine on his forehead, went all the way down, touched the back of his head to the floor and came back up again without spilling a drop!

The Mother of the man from Nazareth asked him to do something about the wine. They were deep in conversation. He seemed to be disagreeing with her. I thought, oh no, not another argument! So I got busy doing the circle dance. The next thing I knew everyone was toasting us and saying, "Taste the new wine. Wonderful deep red wine. See how it sparkles!" My husband's friends didn't know what to think. One of them said he must be an Egyptian magician. Another said he did it because he forgot to bring a gift. My Mother had known him since he was a little boy and she told everyone he was a man of great faith. A truly holy man. I ran up to thank him and tell him how happy he had made my wedding day. My face was all flushed from the dancing and when I began to say thank you he cupped my face in his large hands and said, "Remember little Bride, you were made for joy."

I can never forget that moment. I felt so free, as though my heart were soaring. It was a time like Passover when we remember how the Lord has made us free. And so you see, he has been on my mind all morning as I prepare for the Passover feast.

My husband has just gone out again. He came home to tell me "the winemaker," that's what we called the man from Nazareth, his Mother's name was Mary, but secretly we called him "the winemaker." My husband was upset, he wouldn't tell me everything. I know he wants me to be happy here in Jerusalem. It's such a busy city...so many people. My husband just blurted it out, "The Winemaker was killed to-day!" I've never seen my husband weep before. He said it was a terrible, painful death, too cruel for my ears. He left here very upset. Our gentle Winemaker. So kind and giving. Like my

mother said, a man of faith, a holy man. I just
keep remembering him. I can't even get my
preparations made for the Passover...so I just sit
here.

I poured a glass of wine in his honor and held
it up to the sunlight. In my sorrow I looked at
that deep red color sparkling in the sun and remembered him. Somewhere, somewhere in that
wine is joy. That's what he told me to remember. I think of my own daughter and how she'll
come to me on her wedding night flushed from
the dancing to say goodbye. I'll take her face in
my hands and I'll be seeing him as I say,
"Remember little Bride, you were made for
joy." And she'll look at me with her eyes full of
wisdom and she'll understand. She'll know. Because she has hair the color of new wine.

6.

The Centurion

I was always lucky. I think women could
sense that about me. I'm a winner. I was a Centurion because I looked great in the uniform.
Women say it's the helmet with the plume.
They make a lot of jokes about it, but I'll let you
in on a secret...it's the muscular legs they like. I
had three women in my life and none of them
knew about the other. Like I told you, I'm

lucky. You have a lot of time to think when you guard—figure things out. It's a way to keep things movin'. Gets a little slow, we toss a few dice, tell some stories. You can't let 'em get to you; like at crucifixions. They get a little out of hand at crucifixions. So they like to have big guys like me around in case the folks get too feisty. I look good, keep myself in shape. They don't try anything funny when I'm there.

This last crucifixion I guarded we tossed dice for this guy's robe. It was seamless. I remembered he was one of those false Messiah guys. Riff, raff. We get a lot of 'em. But I was lucky as usual, I won the robe. Like I said, it was seamless; they're worth a little so I took it home. I didn't sleep well that night. The next day I hear the Messiah guy's mother had made the robe. I'd had a good look at her that day. Women usually gather in front of me. I look straight out when I'm guarding, see? A soldier stands tall. I don't concern myself with the guy's face hangin' up there on the cross; that's somebody else's problem. I'm just guardin', like this. Straight out.

So like I said, I had myself a good look at this lady. She's older than the other women I see, but that's not important. What struck me was the way she looked back at me. I figure, I'm the same age and size as her son, but I'm from some other world when it comes to this Messiah stuff. I'm just stuck on how she's lookin' at me so I think: "I wonder what her son would look like in my uniform? Would he look as good as I'm gonna look in his seamless robe?" Two days pass. I'm not sleepin' with this guy's robe in my house. The lady who made the robe knows something about me. That's it. What? I lock the robe in a cupboard, have some more wine, invite one of my ladies over. Nothin' is workin'. This has never happened before, I'm not sleepin', it's gettin' so I don't want to eat. The seamless robe's turnin' into sleepless nights, no beginning, no end. I started losin'...my sense of time. I had to get rid of it. I didn't want it near me.

It was easy enough to find out where she lived. The young guy who answered the door was the same guy I saw standin' with her below the cross. I said, "Uh, here...I thought you might want this," and he calls her to the door. I just wanna get outta there. But she comes with that face of hers, like no woman's face I ever saw before and I'm tellin' ya' she's seein' all of me. Up close is worse; she's seein' me good. She takes my face in her hands and says, "There's something very important he wanted you to know." And I hated myself for bein' speechless in front of a woman. I couldn't even croak out, "What?" And she says in the quietest, most gentle voice I've ever known, "He wanted you to know you are forgiven."

I went home and slept for three days. Nothin's ever been the same. The helmet with the plume, the women, the wine, the image, the job...pieces! Just pieces!

I'm part of somethin' now. It's got no beginning...no end. It was in her face...it was somehow in that robe. It's part of me now.

Like I said, I've always been lucky.

7.

A Maiden and Her Mother

I was 14 when I came to Jerusalem for the first time. I didn't know there was going to be a crucifixion that day. My Mother said I'd have to get used to that if I wanted to come into the City. She talked about how they made the Thief carry his own cross. She had only seen Thieves crucified but I remember hearing about a Slave being crucified who worked in my best friend's house, but I didn't want to see it happen. I had heard enough about how horrible it was. Sounds of it surrounded us. You couldn't help but hear the thump, thump of the heavy cross beam against the cobble-stones. I tried to keep my mind on the beautiful sandals my Mother had bought me. People were everywhere, jeering and yelling a mixture of insults and encouragement as though they were watching a dog race. There were three men carrying their cross beams. Mother said the first of the three had claimed to be the Messiah. People followed after him in a great moving mass as he inched along. As we got to the edge of the pavement to cross the street, I was suddenly separated from my mother. I had never been alone in the city before...terror struck me. She was nowhere to be seen. The crowd was pushing me forward against my will. I looked down at my new sandals and hoped they wouldn't get scuffed; they were beautifully jeweled, my freshly manicured toes fit snuggly into the carved front opening. I remembered thinking about the tiny heel and how it would lift my leg just enough to give it a graceful curve.

The teeming crowd gave one last push...and then...I saw the first man. Terrible thorns were sticking out at frightening angles all over his head. He was soaked with blood and sweat. A soldier's fat arm zoomed out striking him hard across his nose; it temporarily blinded him. In great confusion, struggling for his balance he fell backwards landing on his back with the great cross beam on his chest. He had landed on top of my feet! Right across my sandals. His bloodshot eyes looked directly up at me. There he was on top of my sandals, his eyes burning into my soul. I had never seen...it was as though...he was so close I felt like I was...looking at myself...it was so confusing! My mother's arms slipped round my waist from somewhere behind me, pressing me close, her tears falling on my hands, my tears mingling with hers...our hands all wet and helpless. The blow had been so forceful he could no longer see, yet they jerked him up and whipped him on his way. Blindly, he struggled to focus his eyes back in the direction he had left us as he called out into the air, his words reaching my mother's ears, as well as mine and my own daughter's yet to be conceived: "Daughters of Jerusalem, weep not for me who am innocent, but weep for yourselves and your children."

A Maiden and Her Mother

8.

The Shepherd's Nephew

I wish you could have known my Uncle. He was a wonderful storyteller. A big blustery shepherd who took me to raise when my parents died. He invented a wonderful story for me to explain my parents' death. When I was older I could have learned the exact details of their death, but there was such poetry in my uncle's images, I decided his story was part of my heritage.

I was 18 when I learned my Uncle had died. They told me he had climbed to a high rocky place to rescue one of his lambs. When he reached out for it he fell far down into a deep crevice. They were unable to recover his body. He died alone. I comforted myself knowing he would have liked the part in the story about them not being able to find his body. That would mean there was mystery in his story and he would love being part of a good story.

I remember traveling the hills with him. He had funny names for each of the sheep and he would tear pita bread into tiny figures and arrange them on the rocks for stories he would tell me. In spite of his great love for me, I knew even as a small boy I was never going to become a shepherd. The nights fell to bitter cold temperatures out there on the hills, the dogs barked constantly and the sheep's staring eyes frightened me. When they came close, their bulky shadows made ghostly images and their wet wool dulled the air as they stared at me like frightened blindmen.

When I was about 4 or 5 years old, my Uncle woke me one night in a frenzy. I had never seen him so shaken. "You must stay here alone," he was shouting, "and watch the sheep." There was a great thunderbolt of light; I closed my eyes not to be blinded as he ran away yelling back to me, "Don't be afraid; we're going to see the Messiah!" And with that he and the other two shepherds disappeared. I sat up slowly feeling very alone, trying not to see the sheep's eyes. I had never known the night to be so still. I caught the faint scent of wildflowers on a light breeze and saw the siloutette of the dogs poised as silent sentinels against the moon. In my uncertain voice I called the sheep toward me and watched them mesmerized as they walked forward, the dew glistening off their woolly backs. The thin black line of their mouths seemed drawn up into a grin and their eyes caught the gleam of the stars and permeated the night with peace. I was both frightened and comforted, sure and yet mystified, and though I knew I was awake I felt I was living one my Uncle's stories.

When my Uncle and the other shepherds returned, he told me the story of what they had seen. A new born babe wrapped in swaddling clothes. He wished I might have heard the babe's mother singing. "Oh," I cried, "did she look like my mother? What did she sing?" "Well," he said, "she laid the small babe in a manger and as we looked on his new, rosy face she crooned over and over again ever so softly, 'Jesu, Jesu, Mother's here.'" And just as with the story of my parents' death I believed him, his deep voice booming out facts laced with poetry. And from that night on the story stayed sweet in my memory.

When I was about 38 I went to Jerusalem for the Passover. I was told a man had been crucified that afternoon for claiming to be the Messiah. Some said he had claimed he could destroy the temple and rebuild it in three days. I went out into the street; the people were agitated. They reminded me of the night my uncle had left me on my own for the first time. I was recalling his voice, "We're going to see the Messiah," when lightning struck, causing the afternoon sun to grow dark as midnight. In the darkness I recalled the sheep's eyes staring at me, waiting for me to wake up and take charge of my destiny. The light flashed bright again and I began finding my way toward the curcifixion site. By this time the late afternoon light was fading but I could still make out the sign over the middle cross where they were busy taking the crucified man's body down, the one who'd claimed to be King of the Jews. Just then a slight, wiry man they were calling Joseph approached and beseeched me to help. They must complete their task before the sun set. Hurriedly I lifted my share and carried his twisted body forward; we were almost running. As we swept past a huddled group of women, one who looked older followed our path with her hand crooning softly as we passed: "Jesu, Jesu, Mother's here."

Against all odds we labored, wrapping his body in burial cloths Joseph had provided. I thought of that babe wrapped in swaddling clothes laid in a manger and wondered if they had rushed to that cave as we were rushing to the tomb. When I helped give the last push to the great stone covering the burial entrance I pondered the end to his story. Would his body perhaps never be found? Would the details surrounding his death be embellished? A young man called John announced the task was complete and the small band walked together into the night, leaving me alone in the night. As I turned to leave, I caught the faint scent of wildflowers and noted the soldiers standing guard as though to keep the moon away. I had never known the night to be so still. I took my first step into the waiting darkness and whispered to myself and to my dead Uncle, "Don't be afraid, we're going to see the Messiah."

9.

The Official's Daughter

Do you know what happened to me when I was 12 years old? I died. I did. My Mother doesn't know it but I've collected coins from the children for telling them about it. I would get in terrible trouble if she knew. They say: "Tell us what it was like," and I explain it was like falling down a well. Like the inside of Jacob's well. Everything close and dark. And then I heard a man's voice coming from the top of the well...it came down to me in echos. Like a chant from way up at the top, where there was a tiny pin point of light and the voice called me closer and closer to the light, where his arms were reaching to pull me out. And the next thing I knew I was in my Mother's arms eating sweets and drinking warm goat's milk.

The man from Galilee who called me out of the well didn't stay long that day, but I remember the way he looked at me so lovingly and smiled at me and every part of my body felt joyful. After that my Mother took me to hear him talk many times and I could understand what he was talking about, but what I enjoyed the most was sitting on his lap afterwards and visiting. He always had grape juice stains and olive oil footprints on his robe from the smaller children, and we would all laugh together.

Over and over again when my Mother put me to bed I'd say: 'Tell me again how the man from Galilee called to me,' and she'd say: "He wanted his little girl to get up," and I'd say, 'no...say the word he said. She would laugh and say, "It means, child arise" and I'd say, 'nooooo, say the word the way he said it.' And finally she'd say: "Talitha Koum." Isn't that lovely? My Mother said he was speaking to my heart. That's how I heard him.

I'm here alone tonight because it's been secretly arranged for me to meet three women. One of them is Joanna whose husband works in Herod's palace. She helped me arrange everything. I sneaked out from my room in the dark of early morning. My Mother doesn't know I'm here.

Now I must say out loud why I am here. It's very hard.... The man from Galilee is dead. The man who called to me was crucified. He is buried in Joseph of Aramethia's tomb. The three women are going to anoint him in the morning. They don't know it but before they roll back the stone, I'm going to call him like he called me. Oh not out loud...silently. I'll remind him...He's been through so much. Surely, surely if he said it to himself. "Talitha Koum." Say it to yourself..."Talitha Koum." Say it to yourself, "Talitha Koum." Say it to yourself....

The Official's Daughter

63

Mary M: A Visit
With the Magdalene

Introduction

"Mary M" waits to speak as a staged reading or as a play without props, to be performed by men as well as women. According to the gospels, the Magdalene was cured of seven devils, so it is possible to divide the narrative into as many as seven parts, read by women where it is required and by men where it is appropriate.

The play can be presented in churches, prisons, homes for unwed mothers, in theatres as a fundraiser; any place the Magdalene needs to be and will be welcome. With prayer and preparation this lady of excesses will take you there and bring you back, and a part of you will never be the same again. The play is about change and though most of us shy away from repentance, it really means change. So the key word for performance is energy—something is happening. This lady is no "sit-by-the-fire," she is fire itself.

One is tempted toward extravagant production values: a lavish wig, authentic costume, different colored lights, music. A flute or similar wind instrument playing melodies from the Liber Usualis to divide the scenes is effective. Effective? Yes. Necessary? No. As the play traveled from coast to coast, to Europe and back to the Sanctuary, it became evident that less was more. The Magdalene does best traveling light. A podium, a portable spot, the script, and you are ready.

Enjoy your visit.

Scene 1.
Mary M and Jesus

Everybody thinks he was different—that he had a halo around his head and a clean white robe. Let me picture him for you. You could never have told him apart from any man his age. In fact, in a crowd or from a distance, he'd be lost quickly if you were watching for him. He blended. He loved to blend. He had the chameleon's qualities and long after he left us, I'd be reminded of him whenever I saw those creatures of the desert sand.

Once I saw a chameleon with half the back end of its body missing. This little guy wasn't the least disturbed. He went on quite comfortably with just his head and two front feet, blending with the rocks. Well Rabboni could blend. And it was in the blending where the mystery lay.

He very seldom moved quickly, except when sailing, or whittling or telling a funny story. He'd quickly become the man in his own story. He was a fine mimic. He knew people so well it was second nature to him to imitate and he always could make us laugh along the road... mostly imitating Peter. Peter hated to walk when the roads were hot and he had a way of going up on his toes when the sand got warm. Then he'd run to catch up, shaking the sand from his sandals.

Scene One: Mary M and Jesus

I honestly used to think I'd catch him one day. Maybe he'd forget to blend and I'd see the real man. Mornings especially I used to wake early to watch him. For countless days I'd study his eyes. But the wonder of him increased. He was made for mankind, he used to say, and I can tell you he belonged to us. He was as much for our service as the rocks and ground he laid upon. His coloring, his hair, his eyes—they were the tones of the earth and his body rhythms and heart beats were to the tune of man.

If you stood away from the campfire to watch our group from a distance you could never pick him out. It was only in knowing him and in him knowing me, through time, that I came to know he was indeed the Master!

I guess that's one of the most important discoveries about him I wanted to share with you. Believe me, I've seen a lot of men wake up in the morning and after a few minutes their a-wakening look becomes studied, guarded, pretended. I once saw a man die unexpectedly. Uh huh. He was knifed through a tent as he was having dinner with me. I didn't see who killed him. I only saw him die. Well, let me tell you that's one way to lose weight fast. I couldn't eat for weeks. He didn't say goodbye, excuse me; he didn't even close his eyes; he just died.

Well, that's it, you see, his eyes had the same expression dead as alive. Now that's not saying much for the way he looked when he was alive, but there is an expression in the eyes we put there through our own will. Rabboni's eyes carried the will of the Father and though he said this many times, I only came to understand it through the look I saw in his eyes.

Scene 2
Mary M and Peter

Peter, to watch you try to keep a campfire a-live is more entertaining than a night at the Ar-ena. (laughs) I wonder how your act would look with music. I can't help it, I have to laugh. Oh, Peter the smoke! (she fans and coughs) Why does it matter to you why I'm here? Do you realize how many times you have asked me the same questions? But you do always ask the same questions. All right, you word it different-ly, but you see it's still the same question re-

Mary M

gardless of what order you put the words in. I
don't know if you are stubborn or just rude.
Maybe you are both, but you are such fun it
doesn't matter. Oh...Peter, it is dying for sure!
Why don't I fan the embers and you get the
wood? No, it's perfectly good wood, I brought it
this morning. (she lifts her voice) You know
you forget I have questions for you. Well, first
of all who taught you to build a fire? (he returns) Quick, put the wood on, I'm going blind.
You know, Peter, you're so funny, you always
give the impression you know exactly what
you're doing but you don't fool me for a minute.
There, that looks good. Now, if you promise not
to touch the fire I'll answer anything you ask.

Well, you know my father was wealthy and
my mother was beautiful. My father adored her;
he couldn't give her enough. He worked in Jerusalem and owned many fishing vessels. The
fishermen loved him; he was very fair with
them. Our home was in Bethany. Martha is

older than me—than anybody but she can't help herself. I think she was born old. Lazarus doesn't appreciate my teasing her, but Peter, you've seen her; what would you do with a sister like that? That's true, she is like your mother-in-law.

My back is cold. (she goes to fire, turns around, lifts skirt slightly and warms her backside) Well, as you know, Lazarus was always busy making jokes. You know, Peter, he could teach you some social graces. Well I appreciate you, smoke and all. (picks up stick and pokes at the fire in crouched position) You can imagine how well Lazarus handled my father's accounts in Jerusalem. My father was very pleased with him, and my mother...Ah, my mother, how she loved Lazarus. Yes, anybody would love Lazarus. Well, at any rate, he and my father worked well together in Jerusalem. (throws stick into fire and returns to sit) And Martha, my mother and I had a happy time together in Bethany.

73

Mary M

And now I must tell you something, Peter. Women aren't meant to share this information with men. Are you listening? I can't even see you. Well, Martha developed an illness, it was... a bleeding... so Mother and I stayed close to Martha there in Bethany and during this time my father... Peter, are those tears from my story or the smoke? Where was I? Oh, Magdala. Well, my father loved to hunt. The ship owners enjoyed challenging him so he built the beautiful hunting grounds you saw at Magdala. Mother loved it there. She began to plan gardens and fountains... she had so many plans. The direct sunlight was hard on Martha so she seldom went there. She was comfortable at Bethany. Martha in her nest at Bethany, we'd tease her and she'd reply: "The marsh hen builds her nest on the watery sod; I shall build me a nest 'neath the wings of God."

One evening my mother and father were in the garden studying the plans they had made for a beautiful stone stairway. They had climbed a tall hill where the stones were stacked tight and high like a wall, waiting to be put into place. No one knows how it happened... it might have been a jackal, a hare, a stray fox... but the stones got dislodged and the wall... the whole wall fell on them. The servants found them, but the stones had done their damage.

They both fell with such force... they were separated in their fall... they were completely buried. It took a long time to get their bodies out. My mother's hands... I wish I hadn't seen them... under her nails there was earth and pieces of stone. She must have clawed fiercely to get to my father. Her face, her lovely face was gone, but her hands for some reason, her painted nails... there were only scratches. People don't bleed when they die instantly. Did you know that Peter? Did you know fright can kill people? Maybe in falling. It was so useless and pointless. Two beautiful people, creating a beautiful place, making a view. It's almost funny; their view fell on them.

I was there that evening. I heard the servants, and so, of course, I saw. They carried me inside, but I ran out again and again. I remember howling like a dog. It started someplace here and went into a high pitch.

In a way, I know I went mad. I couldn't bear to think the sun would be so brazen to rise again on Magdala and how dare another flower grow in that garden that claimed those sweet bodies.

Lazarus took care of everything. Martha's health grew worse and I... What about me? What was I going to do? What was I going to find? Answers? Meaning? I can tell you this, Magdala was no longer beautiful to me. I would create my own beauty—with the arts! My friends, the philosophers and actors. And perhaps I might become an actress. The theatre was very near. I would make things beautiful. The grounds, the house, the gardens; there would be music and wisdom; there would be meaning! And I would never have to remember... Peter, look at your fire. It's perfect now.

Scene 3
Mary M and Martha

Well, Martha could quote the Scriptures. How she could quote! I think she memorized them purposely to taunt me. She would never say them to my face though. She was a Greek chorus of one.

She would find a chore for herself in the house and get very busy only a few feet away from me. Then very obsequiously she'd begin her chant.

One of her favorite tricks was to catch me drying my hair. That was good for an hour's worth of quoting. I love to sit in the sun and comb and scent my hair. If you put perfume on the hair while it is still damp and let it dry in the sun, the scent can drive men mad.

Tullus loved to wrap his face in my hair and pull it around for a moustache and do one of the characters he had seen performed in the theatre. He would make me laugh so hard we'd both get tangled in my hair. Sometimes I'd laugh so hard I'd cry from the pain and nonsense.

But with Martha, there was never nonsense. Only what? Concern? Care? No, more of a longing. And I could hear it in her voice. And at that point I hated her for caring about me. My life was full of fun, parties, and the adventure of the stories we would perform at the theatre. And there was much beauty!

My breasts were glorious. Just to look at them put men into ecstacy. I kept my thighs soft with perfumed oil. They were pillows of luxury. My body was a haven of fantasy. Why, I could cover a man's back with my perfumed hair as he lay with me and envelope him with my sensuousness and whispered promises. The quotes I knew to whisper were enticing lessons I learned from Apelles, and, oh, had Martha heard them we'd have had Scripture for 24 hours!

I often wondered just how much she knew about me. How the men made wagers throughout the evening and the winner would spend the night with me. Well, at any rate, there I'd be, completely ignoring her, basking in the sun. But it never bothered her for a minute. And now I must admit to you a secret. Without my knowing it, I began to memorize what Martha quoted to me. I never meant to do it. I fell in love with the words. No, I should say, the sound of them. The sound seduced me. And much later the meaning captured me. How can I... They chased me 'til I caught them. Of course, being an actress words were important to me. And Martha was clever; she loved wisely. The warm sun, the perfumed air. And the words of life:

My beloved lifts up his voice,
he says to me,
"Come then, my love.
my lovely one, come.
For see, winter is past,
the rains are over and gone.
Flowers appear on the earth.
The season of glad songs has come,
the cooing of the turtledove is heard
in our land.
Fig trees are forming their first figs,

blossoming vines give out their fragrance.
Come then, my love,
my lovely one, come!"

81

Scene 4
Mary M and Tullus

I think it was the loneliness that began to change me. But I blame it on the dawn. Having breakfast alone is the ultimate insult. And when I would find myself alone with the dawn I began to be resentful of something I couldn't pin down. Was it the day? The day had such a chance to be glorious; the day was waiting to be admired, to be enjoyed. I was alone in the dawn, a sister to the night. I never fit in a new day; there was no place for me to work my magic, no promises for me to fulfill. I belonged to the darkness with its secrets. And I know them all by heart. My hands, my body speak instinctively in darkness. There is no place for me in the dawn.

(she turns to watch Tullus as he sleeps) Tullus... Tullus... That snore; it is the only time he dares to make a statement. He saves his dreams and fantasies for me. My breasts, my thighs know those desires and we are not impressed. While he is in my bed he is the Caesar, he is the Conqueror. I see to that. He knows I hold his answers. And when the sun comes up he'll swallow those snores and they'll become the whimpers he calls his life. Then he'll creep into the damp dawn and I'll have my warm morning cup and I'll curse the dawn and beg her for my place. But for now, right now, there is no doubt where I belong or who I am. As long as he is satisfied, I am sure. You hear that snoring? That's my vote of confidence. It's almost a purr.

Scene 5

Mary M at the Pool

One night just before sunset I was sitting beside my mother's reflection pool at Magdala. Oh, you would love it there! Just greenery, marble statuary and still waters. The cypress trees reflected in the water are gigantic, bigger than life. The air from the water is cool and soothing. It was cleverly designed. The trees catch the sounds, a stillness captured me. Tiny ripples brought life to my thoughts.

Mary M

I studied the statues my mother had placed there to reflect in the pool. Now if there were three statues and three children, who do you think is placed there for posterity in marble? Humm? (laugh) Naked as the crows we stand. Three wayside stations for the sparrows: Martha, Lazarus and "little Mary." I remember posing. We were all done at three years of age.

First there was Martha holding her grapes. (strikes pose) Then Lazarus standing boldly without a stitch (strikes pose), addressing his body to the world! And "little Mary" (strikes pose) clutching my mother's precious alabaster jar. I remember how the alabaster felt against my naked skin, and I can still hear the artist praising my curls and my ability to sit for long periods, contemplating the colors reflected in the alabaster.

Martha's statue was offering grapes (strikes pose), "busy, busy, busy," and looking back at me to take one. I kept looking at the statues thinking again of my sweet mother's frail beauty and how it had been crushed like Martha's grapes. But the grapes had become wine; what had become of my mother's body? Where was that flesh of my flesh, that bone of my bone? I wondered if she knew how I treasured her alabaster jar? She used to describe the aroma of the oils it contained.

I studied the statues through the ripples and it was odd, but of the three statues reflected there, my statue, looked like a blind child! Well, it must have been because I was looking down at the jar. The many colors reflected in the alabaster had mesmerized me. I remember when I turned the jar the colors would change. While I was thinking about the colors I caught a reflection in the pool and it frightened me. It was myself looking at the child statue and I looked *blind*! I found myself crying: what is it? Why isn't beauty enough? Why is meaning so important? All that is beautiful dies, changes, passes away. And we are left, aren't we, like blind

Mary M

children grasping at dreams, memories and
"might have beens." Am I a blind child who's
become a blind woman? My heart longs to soar
like the cypress. I want to see with my heart.
Where is meaning? Where shall I find it?

Scene 6

Mary M and the

Healer

I began to wake in the middle of the night with my mind racing. It was always at the same time—just before dawn. That hideous time! To avoid my thoughts I began to get up and walk about. This particular morning Tullus had won the wager the night before and so... Tullus was in my bed. Light had begun to invade the room.

Flower petals had been strewn about my bed. Their inviting scent had lured Tullus and me only hours earlier. Now they were crushed and brown. One of them flitted in the air as Tullus snored. I watched it lift and fall to the rhythm of his stale breath. Suddenly I felt suffocated. "Stop invading my life," I longed to scream at the light. "Get out! Leave me to the night."

Tullus rolled over in his drunkenness and a flower petal was stuck to his forehead. That did it! I grabbed my cloak and headed for my reflection pool. It was easier to accept the on-coming light if I could see myself as part of it. The future threatened me. The past haunts me. Is it the present I can't handle?

All of Magdala was still. The servants were fast asleep. Only animals wake at this hour.

Just as I sat down to see my reflection there was a sound, and in an instant I stood again and held my breath in fright. Someone was with me in the garden. Someone was standing next to me. I didn't need the morning light to tell me who it was. I could sense it without looking. It was the man they called THE HEALER!

He was as out of place in my garden as that rose petal on Tullus' forehead. Yet he was there. So simple. Straightforward. Uninvited. Out of place. Standing there in my garden!

The reality made me lightheaded and I sat down against my will. And then He spoke: "Why have you never invited me here?" And he looked steadily at me. Why have you never invited me here? There was only one thing to do... *run*!

I don't know how far I ran, or for how long. But I remember laughing wildly as I ran. What a picture he made. Asking a question like that. Standing there in my garden. What would he have done there? (she laughs hysterically) What could I have done for Him?

My servants found me and brought me home. I could feel the noonday sun burning into fresh cuts on my arms and legs. My cloak was ripped in half, my hair was matted and tangled with leaves and thistles. I had exhausted myself.

My servant bathed me and put me to bed. And when I woke from a deep sleep, I knew what I had to do.

Scene 7
Mary M and Simon

I found my mother's alabaster jar beside my bed. It had been there since I was three. My mother had presented it to me to keep on the night that my statue was unveiled. In a way the jar had become a symbol to me all these years. The outside so beautiful to see... all the colors. The coolness of the outside so refeshing to my touch. But the inside. Oh, the precious inside.

Waiting to be given. Dark inside all these years, waiting in darkness... waiting to be given.

I sent my servant away. And slowly and deliberately I began to undo my perfumed hair. I remember my mother's hands unbraiding it as she prepared me for bed as a little girl, singing sweet songs about the moon and the stars. And for the first time there was no violence in my remembrance of her hands. It was as though she were there at that moment helping me unbraid and comb. I saw the light from my candle reflect in my hair and I recalled the sunlight. And Martha's chants of the Scriptures:

> Come to me, my love
> My lovely one, come.

I took a lamp in one hand and in my cloak carefully and lovingly wrapped my precious alabaster. Then, without ever looking back, I left my Magdala and headed in the unknown darkness... for the house of Simon.

Scene 8
Mary M and Matthew

Matthew, why doesn't it concern you that Judas is stealing? You saw what happened when he counted the money and you said nothing. Yes, it's his job, but all he has to do is count. When did stealing become his work? I was sitting here, you were standing there, we both saw the silver before he began totaling. Matthew, maybe you're not aware of it, but this is the third time he has singled us out and counted the money in front of us. Just you and me. He reminds me of a wild dog bringing dead prey into the house. I've watched you, Matthew; you pretend to ignore him, but he searches your eyes as he counts. What does he want?

You were the tax collector. I remember seeing you in action. You don't need to touch the coins to count them, do you? In fact, from the stories I've heard, you could total a man's wealth by the cut of his garment and the heel of his sandal. If I sound angry it's because I am. Because the money does not belong to Judas, it belongs... why am I shouting?

You know the money is a common fund; it is ours... all of ours. It is as much yours as it is mine but I'm shouting and you are ignoring everything. It goes quickly enough without watching a brother steal it!

When I think of selling the castle at Magdala and bringing the money here—my heart was soaring with purpose. The money was to be put into the hands of the Master. What is he doing with my money? Why must I be forced to look at him? Matthew, please answer me.

I don't want to be angry. I think I know but I don't want to be forced to say it. I just said the money was mine, didn't I? I still claim it, don't I?

Why didn't you stay in charge of the funds, Matthew? You could have done it so easily. I know you must have brought a great deal when you came, we are the only two who could have brought so much. Matthew, tell me... it should be easy for you to talk to me. I know you're upset. Judas would upset anybody. Look at me, my fists are clenched.

What is it? What are you reminded of? Shall I hold your hand? Well, look at yourself, you're wringing your hands. Where are you when I'm washing the clothes? I could use such force. Come and sit. There, now.

Do you know I remember you coming to the twilight symposiums at Magdala? You dressed so beautifully then I couldn't help but notice you. Of course, I like to think I looked a little better then myself. One thing I do know, I smelled a lot sweeter. I saw you laugh.

You were always very quiet then. I think all you cared about was money and finding ways... (he jumps up)... Oh, that got a reaction! I was right?

Matthew, whatever there was about you I found attractive then, it is even more so now. And look at you in your raggy cloak. There was something about you I loved, but you spent it. Oh, it's good to see you laugh.

Matthew dear, what holds me here is what holds you. It is why you are attractive to me. It certainly isn't the money. It is your vision. It is the way you live the Master's words. I know it isn't easy for you. I've seen you choke on the food and massage your bruised feet. And most of all I have seen you stare at my bracelet.

Yes, it is pure gold. I'm certain you could tell me its worth. It is all I have kept, Matthew. Because... because... my body is my money. You know that. You knew about the evenings at Magdala. My body could settle any dispute. All right, I'll say it. Judas stares at the bracelet because he has guessed my weakness... if I am ever pushed too far I still have my bracelet. How can I ever be sure of myself again? I'm trying Matthew, but I must keep the bracelet. I can't let go of everything at once. Oh Matthew, hold my hands. I feel like a weak fool... talk to me, tell me anything. Tell me how you cheated... Matthew!... That's a great deal of money! I must say, your cheating was more sophisticated than your cloak.

Oh, you're getting all upset again. That was yesterday. Judas is cheating today. He knows about our past. He realizes you can no longer bear to touch the money.

Look at it this way, Matthew. I cheated myself, you cheated others, he's cheating all of us. He's the only one who isn't holding back. The joke is on us, Matthew. If we've managed to change our lives, he knows there's hope for himself.

He is seeking us out to show him the way. We could understand; we've been there. What? Why am I wringing my hands?... Oh!

Scene 9
Mary M and Judas

So you see, it was impossible to hate in the Master's presence. If I was to remain, to stay near him, to know the meaning I had longed for, I would have to come to terms with Judas. What did he want? What was he all about?

I'll tell you this, he was bright. He never stopped multiplying our funds. Where Matthew had let go of money, Judas had clutched it. And made all totals fit the law!

He did not have a sense of humor—seldom smiled. The only time I saw his teeth was when he bit a coin. So intense. It wore me out to sit next to him. It was a task to begin to know him.

He was not a Galilean and this separated him from the others. He was a city man, not much for wine and conversation. He was a brooder. Why couldn't I handle him alone? I've made love to men who repelled me far more than him.

I began to study him in the Master's presence. He was the... (interrupts herself)... Oh, I forgot to tell you, he blinked a lot. I don't know why. He would listen intently, consider, then... blink, blink, blink! He looked like a camel with sand in his eyes.

He was tall and bony. And you noticed he had a long neck with dull soulful eyes. Because the others ignored me subtly, very subtly, I could understand Judas' aloofness. But it was

Mary M

easy to see that the loneliness was difficult for him. (she appraches Judas and sits) Judas, I sit beside you, I sing for you, I serve you food. You never speak to me. We could be friends, you know. I have no more expensive oils to pour a-way. You can't still be angry about that?... I could listen. I would like to know what you think, you can trust me. We are here for each other, Judas. I'm not going to judge your thoughts... just share them. Judas, it pains me to see you think so deeply and never speak. (she walks away from Judas quietly and comes back to the audience)

Knowing Judas was a slow beginning. And a painful end. And when Judas came to his end... well, let me tell you how I came to be there... (she walks far upstage)

One night, after many walks and talks by fire-light, Judas had gone with me to gather fresh wood. We would cover it to keep it dry for a breakfast fire. I had spread my cloak to wrap it.

I wasn't looking at him, I was thinking about what he had just told me.

Judas longed for love among us. He did not find among the disciples the love the Master showed to us. And this puzzled him, gnawed at him. He sensed deeply a vague division among us. This was not the proper atmosphere for the Messiah! Would one of us trade places with the Master? Give our life for him? If he was indeed the Messiah, should there be a plan so Rabboni might have a public way to save himself? Should he, Judas, provide the way?

According to the law, Judas had a plan. But he was too frightened. He loved the Master, he longed to have him identified as the Messiah to the Sanhedrin. And he was proud of this plan.

He watched me fold the wood in my cloak and wrap it. Then suddenly he fell on his knees in front of me and made me promise him something. It was a frantic, fitful request, and for a moment his eyes blazed with pleading. And he bellowed out like a wild animal, "Will you take care of me?" It didn't make any sense. If I'd known at that moment what he was talking about....

But on the night Rabboni was led away, nobody thought to look for Judas. Nobody cared to look. Our thoughts were wild that night. We were all so frightened.

I didn't run away that night. In fact the one time I ran from Rabboni in my garden was the last time in my life I ever turned my back to flee. After meeting him face to face nothing could ever frighten me again.

And Tullus had often come near and bargained. Roman soldiers threatened. Old lovers tempted. But the only fear I ever knew was the certain knowledge that the emptiness could return at any moment!

(walks to new spot)

Well, on that night I went alone to a place Judas had often described to me. I took a blade. No one told me. But I took a blade. I took it not to defend myself, but to free Judas. And I was right. I knew where I could find him. There was a Redbud tree near a wall on the left side of a hill. It was dark by the time I got there. (sees him) His body was still warm. But a grotesque rigor mortis had set in. His eyes and tongue hung like unfurled banners beseeching me to keep my promise to take care of him.

I climbed the tree easily in the moonlight. I talked to him as I climbed to steady myself:

"I'm not going to judge you, Judas. You shared your thoughts with me. We're here for each other.

"But to sell him, Judas... give him a kiss... I know about those things.

105

Mary M

"What about me, Judas, would I give my life for the Master?... I can't let go of everything at once... Isn't loving enough?

"Why did you ask me here, Judas? I don't want to touch you... (guttural sound, bent over as though retching).

(slowly comes up) "I promise not to judge you, Judas... Let me be the one disciple who could love you in your sin."

Then I realized, looking down on that rigid body, just how securely he had clung to his dream. And as he fell free of the rope I realized, *he* had perhaps loved Rabboni the most. But his allegiance in the end went to his dream, and his love remained as twisted as his body.

I sat a long time in the tree searching for the bond I held with this strange man... the struggle. That was our bond... the struggle. It's there, isn't it, until the end.

Scene 10
Mary M and Martha

Martha, I would feel better if I could tell you something. Will you listen quietly and not comment? Ahhh, not a word! Please Martha, it's terribly important. No, it won't take long. Why must you measure everything? Weigh my words? Count them?

There's such a difference between you and Lazarus when I long to share my heart. Well, I suppose the difference is... with Lazarus, I can tell him every thought. And my words are accepted, usually with a laugh or two. And what I think is good enough... exciting, to be shared, wonderful to his ears. With you, it better be good!

Well, the better part of me is foolishness, Martha. I thrive on the unexpected or I'd go mad. Listen to me, I wanted to very calmly tell you something. Let me try again... Uh... (waits...stares at her) You must stop the weaving, Martha. Put it down. (waits) Thank you.

Do you remember the day you decided to ask for a healing? Well, I thought you were mad. I told myself: "She'll get into that crowd and be crushed, contaminated, insulted, trampled by horses..." who knows what could happen to you? Frankly, I thought your mental powers were getting weak from losing so much blood. I thought most of all I owed it to you to protect you. But, *from a distance!*

And so at noon my servant and I watched you from the hill above the olive grove. I want you to know I saw what happened, Martha. You didn't even speak to him. Ahhh... not a word, you promised! (very loud) You crawled behind him like a whipped dog to lick his sandal. You, Martha with the mighty tongue, merely touched his robe.

I didn't mean to make you cry. Oh, what's happening? I'm saying it all wrong. Let me try again. My life now as a disciple is because of you, Martha... and... I both hate you and love you because of it. I had no idea you could humble yourself so. When I was little, Martha, you knew how to say anything... everything! And as I grew I continued to look for your words... until I grew old enough to think for myself and then, your words no longer sought, came as stumbling blocks, bumping together in my brain. So you see on that fateful day that you were healed, it came as a shock; you asked for it without words. "Martha the mouth," silenced by her need.

That you would be healed by a mere touch! It was the gesture, Martha. I wanted you to know, your touch of his garment was really *you* touching my heart. (raises voice) Now, please, when I finish, just let me walk away. I couldn't bear it if you spoke to me... (softly)... I know now not everything needs to be put into words. Not everything needs to be said. Oh, Martha, it was so simple. You, of all people, doing such a simple act.

Not me; not Mary! I must weep at his feet. Dry tears with my hair. *Wail* for forgiveness. Be surrounded by an audience. And all must see and hear and witness my belief. Nothing so simple as getting lost in the crowd and believing in a tiny touch of the fingertips. I must be seen and heard and felt. My sins are BIG!

(softly) Oh, Martha, I'm no good at anything simple. (on her knees) But I have come to ask forgiveness. I brought you something in this box. When you open it after I've gone you'll find... it is... my hair. I cut it off... I wanted you to have it.

Scene 11
At the Cross and
Resurrection

Have you ever seen your life as a circle? I used to think of that when I looked at my bracelet. Once I followed the Master, birth, death, life seemed without beginning or end. With Rabboni there was no sense of time. Except when he left us. There seemed to be... well... I should explain. None of us thought he was going to die.

He said he would never leave us, he was with us to the end. We were not ready for him to die. But I've told you enough of death. I could not bear to tell you of his. I know how many times you've thought about it. I will tell you this, I stayed until the end. The crowds had all gone home. Another phony Messiah finally silenced.

(turns to look at top of cross) Buzzards were circling the sign above his head. (runs to cross—hands up, lights flash once) "The King of the Jews" (drops hands) "is quiet!" (walks away) One of them tripped over a skull as he left. The dull thud reminded me how all the earth and sky stunk of death!

There was his mother, John, Joseph of Aramathea, his mother's cousin, Nicodemus and myself. And you know the details of his last words. But I wish you might have been there as we took him down. (arms outstretched) As the men lowered him from the final step of the ladder, I ached to hold him. To wipe his face, cover his sweet nakedness... But at that instant his mother called out... "Mary, sing!"

Sing? I had begun to *shake*. John was working quickly and the outline of his mother's face against the setting sun gave me new strength. Suddenly she was rocking her dead son. (walk away) I stood away against the raging colors of twilight and began a lullaby I had once heard him sing to a dead child.

Joseph wrapped quickly and I sang into a dying light.

(Walks to new spot) I don't know if you've noticed, but I don't wear my bracelet anymore. I put it on the night I left for Simon's house and I never took it off 'til the morning we left for Rabboni's tomb. You'll never guess who has it now. But you will understand better why the Master felt I might want to keep it.

Mary M

(walk to spot and step) As we approached the tomb before it was light, the other women stopped abruptly about half a mile from the entrance. I didn't say anything because it was easy to see why they didn't want to go on. There were seven Roman guards, three on each side and one directly in front of the entrance. The men had told us we were fools to think they'd let us by. I won't lie to you and tell you I was not frightened. I was more than afraid, because I recognized the tallest Roman at the entrance.

I knew that slight slump to the shoulders, those muscled arms. I knew too much to stop walking, so I went on alone. As I approached the tallest and stood directly in front of him, he took a long gulp of wine... and spit in my eyes! (Right arm quickly over eyes) The stench of the stale wine ran down my face and as I reached to wipe it away, I undid my gold bracelet. (hold right arm out)

"Tullus, you've often admired this. Will you have it so that I might pass?"

The rest is difficult to recall exactly, but when I entered the tomb it was empty. There were pieces of the shroud about the floor and the light seemed to be bouncing off the inside of the white walls as though the sun was coming up from the floor. (bent over and fumbling) I stumbled outside to adjust my eyes and an old gardener was standing there. At least he seemed old. His cloak was covering his face and he was standing directly in front of the rising sun.

I felt like a very old beggar woman all bent up peering blindly at the faceless creature. I clutched the side of the rock and blurted out, (arm shading eyes) "Where have they taken my Lord?"

And the faceless creature said: (arm away, hands either side of eyes) "Mary."

Without seeing his face I knew who called my name. (standing) "Rabboni!" And his face came out of the hood, as a new born babe peeps from

115

its swaddling clothes... all new, perfection, just born!

I dove for his feet. And there in the dawn, the rosy dawn, a voice called: "Do not cling to me, I have yet to go to my Father... Go... (hands high in the air)... tell the others what you've seen." (drop hands)

(very soft) That was all. It was as simple as the morning I found him in my garden. And as I told you, once I saw his eyes, I never turned back.

(one step to the audience)

Through the timelessness of a circle of time I have come to do what I was called to do. He told me to go straight to you. And now that I have found you, I tell you... I HAVE SEEN THE LORD.

(Blackout)